Contemporary Poetry

CONTEMPORARY POETRY
———— I Am Blessed ————

BY
Christian Ofosu

RESOURCE *Publications* • Eugene, Oregon

CONTEMPORARY POETRY
I Am Blessed

Copyright © 2025 Christian Ofosu. All rights reserved. Except for brief quotations in critical publications or reviews, no part of this book may be reproduced in any manner without prior written permission from the publisher. Write: Permissions, Wipf and Stock Publishers, 199 W. 8th Ave., Suite 3, Eugene, OR 97401.

Resource Publications
An Imprint of Wipf and Stock Publishers
199 W. 8th Ave., Suite 3
Eugene, OR 97401

www.wipfandstock.com

PAPERBACK ISBN: 979-8-3852-5021-9
HARDCOVER ISBN: 979-8-3852-5022-6
EBOOK ISBN: 979-8-3852-5023-3

VERSION NUMBER 06/06/25

To
My Dear Readers
with Love

Contents

Introduction | ix

1. Our *Home* | 1
2. Demon Days | 4
3. Victims | 6
4. Exaltation | 9
5. Dining with the Enemy | 12
6. Bondage | 14
7. The Saints | 17
8. My Friends | 19
9. Lonely Man | 22
10. Grace, I'm Sorry! | 24
11. Let My Enemies Speak! | 26
12. Goodbye, Utsunomiya! | 28
13. #202 | 30
14. The Rising Sun | 32
15. Kings and Kinsmen | 34
16. Citizen | 37
17. In the Wilderness | 39
18. The Fall of the Enemy | 41
19. Ayumi | 44
20. The Great Escape: A Lament for Lost Worlds | 46
21. Matchmaker | 48
22. My Reign | 50
23. Takahara | 52
24. Mitsukari (Ayumi) | 54
25. Human Harvest | 56
26. Reflections | 58
27. Manzanar | 60
28. Baby King | 63
29. No More Evidence | 65
30. Re-Union | 67
31. The Last Apostle | 69
32. Disclaimer of a Witness | 71
33. I Am Blessed | 73

Introduction

WELCOME, READER, TO CONTEMPORARY *Poetry*. This collection is an exploration, a conversation, a journey through the multifaceted landscape of human experience. Within these pages, you'll find poems that grapple with the grand narratives of our time—the shifting tides of international politics, the enduring scars of war and the fragile hope of peace, the evolving tapestry of love and feminism, and the complex legacy of African history and politics. But you'll also find the deeply personal: reflections on spirituality, responses to pressing social issues, and glimpses into my own experiences and beliefs.

These poems are born from a desire to understand, to question, and to connect. They are an attempt to give voice to the complexities of the world around us and to the inner world we each carry within. From global conflicts to the quiet moments of introspection, I've sought to capture the raw emotions, the nuanced perspectives, and the enduring questions that shape our lives.

You won't find forced rhymes or predictable rhythms here. The poems in this collection are primarily written in free verse, a form that allows for a natural and authentic voice, mirroring the rhythms of thought and speech. My aim has been to create a space where ideas and emotions can unfold organically, inviting you, the reader, to engage with the poems on a deeper level.

This book is not intended to provide easy answers. Instead, it offers a series of reflections, observations, and provocations, inviting you to consider your own perspectives on the themes explored within. Whether you find yourself drawn to the political landscapes, the intimate portraits of love and loss, or the spiritual inquiries woven throughout, I hope these poems spark conversation, ignite your imagination, and leave you with something to ponder long after you've turned the final page.

Brief commentaries are provided for each poem, enabling readers to expand or tailor them to their specific recreational or educational needs.

I am deeply grateful for the divine inspiration that guided the creation of these poems. This collection has been a journey, and I am thankful for the support and encouragement that brought it to life.

Thank you for joining me on this journey. I invite you now to step into the world of these poems.

Our *Home*

Let no man pride himself under the sun,
Lest he become simple and oblivious of his threatened life.
Let no man claim to be the master of his own life,
For he cannot control even a single thread of his hair.
Let no household behave like the lion,
For he has no shield in the den he lives;
Holes abound in his professed fortified *h*ouse.

Ephemeral joy we all share;
Perpetual sorrow, always in the offing.
Today it is the quake;
Tomorrow it is the flood;
The bigger next, our self-made destruction;
Greedily scrambling for the earth's riches, now our woes;
Incessant pollution, threats and deadly wars abound.

There is no sweetness on this earth!
Life is short
In our only *h*o*m*e.
The winds, the predators, all eye the nest,
That its contents will they voraciously consume.
We quake and tremble at what will come next,
And who will be next.

Pray for the peace of Jerusalem,
For the terror, the horror still hangs in the skies!
Friendship ceased; hatred spread fast;

Toasts for wars in secret chambers, so common.
The *h*ouse of the world, weak in its word;
It ails, wails at its shaky feet.
Its fading voice can only be heard afar.

Our tilted *h*ouse, nearing its fall.
Crazy military rivalries and contests, a boom to the doom;
Vain pride, hatred and the fear of the perceived enemy,
Excuses for attack and defense.
But insecurity, the result of massive security.
The first and the second world wars in the past were sample horror scenes;
Armageddon, let no man call for it,
For Sodom and Gomorrah will be the preferred choice.

Oh, Rachel who'll save your children
In these turbulent days!
Tears cease to flow,
Because they have over-stretched their limits.
Agonies, man's daily woes,
Forming his thoughts and images.
A moment delayed, things will tear apart.

Doomsday clock ticks in cautious intervals,
Bit by bit counting man's few minutes left on earth;
A warning to the living to save our dear souls;
No Old Big Ben's fancy that we can smile;
A clutch at our only *h*o*m*e, quicker the safer.
But no one's business to return it safe;
Reverence for riches and super powers, vanity to our cause.

Radical search for new home beyond our skies,
Escape to Mars or the Moon?
Derision to our Maker and deception to ourselves!

We can't fly to leave our *home*; we're neither Albatross nor Arctic Tern.
A mend to our thrashed mesh will surely keep us safe,
For there is no place to live
Than this troubled *home*.

Commentary:

The poem "Our *Home*" presents a sobering reflection on the human condition, emphasizing the fragility of life and the destructive potential of human folly. The central theme is the urgent need for peace and unity in a world teetering on the brink of self-destruction.

The poet employs a variety of literary devices, including vivid imagery, symbolism, and rhetorical questions, to convey his message. The diction is both simple and profound, accessible to a wide audience while still provoking thought. The use of biblical allusions, such as the reference to Rachel, adds depth and historical resonance to the poem.

"The house of the world, weak in its word" in stanza 4, line 5, is a metaphor for the ineffectiveness of global governing bodies like the United Nations. These bodies are so weak and helpless that they cannot do much to help save the world.

The moral lesson inherent in the poem is clear: humanity must prioritize peace, compassion, and environmental stewardship. The poem serves as a cautionary tale, urging readers to recognize the destructive consequences of war, greed, and environmental degradation. It calls for a collective effort to heal the wounds of the past and build a more harmonious future.

Demon Days

During the demon days,
When men were beasts, hearts prim with greed and wickedness,
Trespassing frontiers of lands, rivers and seas;
Gun in hand
To plunder and steal what they'd not labored,
Even from the innocent poor.

During the demon days,
When the wicked with prying eyes,
Searching every nook of the earth,
Raping virgin lands of their riches,
Snatching and annexing lands near and afar,
That they'd be richer and their victims poorer.
The devil's children, dealers in their own, same humankind;
Easy and quick riches, their only goal.
Not wisdom, not bravery, but sheer greed and wickedness!
A people professed so civilized,
Robbers on rampage; killings and atrocities, their very poor.

During the demon days,
The greedy, through mischief and tricks,
Prodded the innocent to part with his lots,
Possessing what did not belong to them;
Corrupt hearts, envious eyes, murderous hands
Dipped deep in the blood of the innocent poor!
Treacherous predators, professed enlightened and models,
Your very crude, insensitive acts betray your claim.

Chaos and confusion, the footprints of your paths;
Indelible scar left on the world's poor;
Chameleons—they change to suit the weather
In pursuit of the innocent poor.
What their victims wish to remember no more,
The proud, with champagne, give it a quick, happy, ceremonial grace.
Change in hearts?
A sign of remorse?
No, a sign of pride of their darkest past.
From generation to generation, same hearts, same blood, same people.
Centuries' atrocities'll surely breed centuries' retribution;
Measure for measure,
A natural rule!

Commentary:

The poem "Demon Days" offers a scathing indictment of human greed, exploitation, and violence. The central theme revolves around the destructive nature of unchecked ambition and the cyclical nature of history.

The poet employs vivid imagery and powerful language to depict the horrors of war, colonialism, and oppression. The diction is stark and direct, emphasizing the brutality and inhumanity of the actions described. The use of phrases like "demon days" and "devil's children" reinforces the moral condemnation of those who perpetrate such atrocities.

The moral lesson of the poem is clear: unchecked greed and power lead to suffering and destruction. The poet warns that history repeats itself and that the consequences of past actions will inevitably be felt by future generations. The poem serves as a reminder of the importance of empathy, justice, and the pursuit of peace.

Victims

Well done, Oh Gallant Warriors!
Who fought the battle against the perpetrators.
The battle that snatched the royal blood;
The blood that resisted the illegal occupation and
Exploitation for countless seasons.
But you came victorious in the middle of the age.
But they rose again with more wickedness and insensitivity.
The thieves who came into the Holy Land,
Thieves who turned themselves into saintly masquerades,
Wearing the skin of lambs.
The masquerades who came in the name of religion and sanctity,
Purging our sanctuary into a perpetual sanctum,
Where peccable would be impeccable and unholy, holy.
Their outward disposition was white and inviting,
But their inward selves, that of wolves—
Hatred, pride, envy, deceit and destruction,
And hiding in the holy cassock they wittingly
Deceived our forefathers, whose convictions and
Customs made them welcome them happily into their once sanctuary.
With pleasure, they plundered treasures into unknown lands.
They callously and wittingly bullied our fathers into
Accepting what was wrong.
With their chalices they forced into the throats
Of our fathers the venom of acquiescence.
Our fathers became like the blind, for they could not see,
They became like the dumb, for they could not speak,
For all these were caused by holy purgation by the false saints.

As if that was not enough,
The perpetrators continued with their abominable acts.
The able-bodied men were bundled like firewood
    into sea-going vessels.
But what happened to the resistant royals?
They were subjected to an avalanche of human agonies;
Some battered and others slaughtered in the face of fellow royals
Like animals slaughtered for the sacrifice of the gods.
Blood streaming down like the fountain of a mountain.
"But if salt loses its taste, what is its use again?
It's poured down and trampled upon, for it has no use again,"
They thought with pleasure.
Such was the fate of the royals.
Their bodies thrown into deep seas.
"Let's feed the fish with these nutritious mammals,"
They thought with happiness.
Those who remained acquiesced and calm were not left to their fate.
They were spat upon, dragged and battered.
Nothing good awaited them during their forced journey to Golgotha.
It was all misfortune, bitterness, diseases, and death.
And what happened to the beautiful maidens?
They were raped and stripped of their virginity and honor;
They were forced to give birth to accursed children,
So that even if the perpetrators left,
Their blood on the land would continue to finish the
    unfinished deeds.
Oh, the land of riches!
Oh, the land of treasures and honey!
Oh, the land of peace and harmony!
My children have been subjected to seemingly eternal servitude;
My children have become victims—a situation not created through
    their own faults.
I've been reaped of my treasures and riches, thus leaving me bare
    and empty.

Today, I've been turned into penury, decrepitude and decadence.
Can I regain my riches and glory?
Behold, I can see *Odomankoma* re-animating me like
   a rejuvenated river.

Commentary:

The poem "Victims" is a powerful and poignant exploration of historical injustice and oppression. The central theme is the suffering and resilience of a people who have been subjected to colonization, exploitation, and cultural genocide.

The poet uses vivid imagery and emotive language to convey the brutality and cruelty of the oppressors. The diction is both lyrical and stark, highlighting the contrast between the beauty of the victimized culture and the ugliness of the crimes committed against it. The use of biblical allusions, such as the reference to the "holy cassock," adds depth and historical resonance to the poem.

The moral lesson of the poem is a call for justice and remembrance. The poet urges readers to acknowledge the suffering of the victims and to work towards a future free from oppression and inequality. The poem serves as a reminder of the importance of preserving cultural heritage and resisting forces that seek to destroy it.

Exaltation

Hail him! Hail him! Hail the great one!
Limann, whose words soothe the heart of the angry.
But whose might makes enemies' strongholds shake.
The giant who has come for the continuity of the work of
    his predecessors.
It isn't by any man's scheming that you are a Chief today,
But by the grace of Odomankoma.
Odomankoma gives you wisdom, humility and love.
May his umbrella of protection be upon you forever!
Blessed are those who bless you.
But he who prays evil against you,
May his own prayer be an accursed necklace around his neck.
May he taste the bitter punishment of the Great One!
Long live Limann! Long live the people of Ghana!

May you sleep in eternal peace!
Yaa Asantewaa, who resisted the conquer of the enemy;
You who defied all orders in order to defend the defenseless
    and the kingdom;
You without a scabbard, who had the spirit of those with scabbards;
You who could withstand the strength and wrath of men;
It was not your war, but you fought gallantly;
It was not your battle, but you waged it fiercely.
You wore the heart of men;
You were like the wounded lion in the battlefield!
The greatest warrior ever known in the life of our great kingdom.
Although you've joined the ancestors,

Your blood and spirit still live with us.
Your spirit continues to protect and guide us in all our endeavors.
Well done! Well done! Well done!

Woe! Woe! Woe!
Since the dawn of days, sorrow has been our constant companion.
From the hand of the shaper, shadow was wrought,
And by that shadow, the shaper was undone.
If not death, you should have been with us,
Osagyefo Kwame Nkrumah whose bravery and power redeemed the people
From the tentacles of the enemy.
Chief whose spirit of understanding and adroitness
Triggered the awareness of the occupation and removal of the enemy;
Chief who caused the cessation of the exploitation by the drone;
The only Chief we knew in the beginning of our kingdom;
You made known our kingdom to the seven worlds.
Even when your kinsmen were in an abyss of despair,
You became a catalyst and rekindled their hope;
You wiped their tears of bitterness.
Although you've gone, you still reign in spirit;
You only became a victim,
But you never became a lost soul.
Condolence!   Condolence!   Condolence!

Commentary:

The poem "Exaltation" is a tribute to three significant figures from Ghanaian history. The first part celebrates the leadership of Dr. Hilla Limann, praising his wisdom, strength, and dedication to the people of Ghana. The second and the third parts mourn the loss of a traditional African leader, Yaa Asantewaa, and the first president of the Republic of Ghana, Dr. Kwame Nkrumah, whose bravery and wisdom are extolled.

The central theme of the poem is the interplay between human power and divine will. The poet acknowledges the limitations of human leadership and the ultimate sovereignty of a higher power. The diction is both lyrical and solemn, reflecting the profound respect and admiration for the individuals being honored.

The moral lesson of the poem is to honor and remember those who have made significant contributions to society. The poet emphasizes the importance of preserving the legacies of great leaders and learning from their examples. The poem also serves as a reminder of the transient nature of life and the inevitability of death.

Dining with the Enemy

Little minds! Little minds!
Simplemindedness has made you stuck thick at your enemy's table.
You've lain under the dining table for too long a time;
A scorn of the wicked, the old enemy;
A quick thought, little labor and bread'll overflow on your table.

Little minds! Little minds!
Rich, vast fields abound, metals and precious stones are gifts,
But cup in hand at every door;
A piteous pittance, a great win for the day;
Remnants of his breakfast, a sumptuous meal for your dinner.

Little minds! Little minds!
Is it forgiveness or forgetfulness?
No eyes to see? No ears to hear?
Awake! Make haste, think twice
Before the killer of your dreams causes your perfect fall.

Little minds! Little minds!
Why froth yourselves in this flirtation, the unholy marriage?
Remember your bitter past, the gruesome, horrifying acts,
And you'll identify your common enemy
Before he makes you a permanent laughing stock.

Little minds! Little minds!
In your own yards great banquets are lavished on your enemy.
Out of fear or show-offs?

Diseases and starvation consume your flock.
Traditional worship of the lesser-god, now over.

Little minds! Little minds!
Greed, waste and self-pleasures, your very lots;
Always servants and beggars of your enemy.
In the midst of abundance, poverty reins;
Observe the ant and learn his ways, and bread'll be ever plentiful
    on your table.

Commentary:

The poem "Dining with the Enemy" is a scathing critique of a people who have become complacent and subservient to their oppressors. The central theme is the importance of self-respect, independence, and resilience.

    The poet's message is conveyed through striking imagery and powerful language. The diction is sharp and direct, emphasizing the absurdity of the situation. The use of repetition, particularly the phrase "Little minds," reinforces the central idea and creates a sense of urgency.

    The moral lesson of the poem is a call to action. The poet urges the reader to break free from the cycle of dependency and to reclaim his dignity. The poem serves as a reminder of the importance of self-sufficiency, resourcefulness, and the pursuit of justice.

Bondage

In my cradle began the surveillance, the battle unknown;
On the paths of deadly, hidden traps I trod unknown,
That I might fall to my enemies' joy.
Where wouldn't I go that I wouldn't meet an enemy?
Where wouldn't I pass that I wouldn't encounter persecution?
Public enemy, hated more than the world hates Jews!
The day of my handcuffing,
Heaven mourned; Satan rejoiced;
Light disappeared; darkness'd befallen me.
Alone in million's hands; ominous life had begun.
Chains binding wrists, waist and feet,
Gagging rags in mouth, locks sealed them.
Not arrest by a warrant, but a hostage by the terror.
My captors whispering eerie sounds: insults, lies, threats of death,
Subjecting me to affliction and disgrace;
Clothed me with a cloth of shame.
In the streets, shops, malls and halls,
Overt mockery and scorn did I suffer.
My scoffers broadened their faces in glee,
In a perfect style to match a fool's display;
Entertainment worth its fun!
In their wisdom and thoughtfulness, the greatest fun under the sun;
Never tired of this sweet act.
A strange being from a strange land!
But a false posture, deception to my scoffers;
A victim of circumstances indescribable.
My body weak and wretched,

My breath in occasional flow;
Was I dead?
No, in transition, a living dead!
In solitude I moaned and groaned of my fate;
Saturated with affliction, disgrace and despair overflowing,
Many times, I thought: death profitable, life not worth living!
A swift embrace into Heaven's bosom,
That I might have relief and rest eternal.
But bitter potion not so sweet a juice,
That I might gulp to end my breath.
I tried to find a way to my freedom,
But not a match to my captors.
Out of true heart did I pray to my God.
Not a season long was I alone; He was with me.
In His infinite love, the stronger hand worked to my cause.
Let Heaven rejoice; once a slave freed forever!
The fool says in his heart: there's no God!
A folly, a joke, absolute protection self-denied.

Father, you're with me in my distress and hopelessness;
You redeemed my life and destiny;
You helped me to regain my freedom and health;
A fresh, happy beginning have you bestowed on me,
And in abundance shall I enjoy my pleasure and wealth.
But history's duty to shelve and recount my bitter past.
Let the world have your heart,
That on earth be no more pain or hurt.
If I can pay you in turn,
Endless thanks do I faithfully return.

Commentary:

The poem "Bondage" is a harrowing account of a person's experience with captivity and suffering. The central theme is the resilience of the human spirit in the face of adversity.

The poet uses stark descriptions and powerful language to convey the depths of the protagonist's despair and the brutality of his captors. The diction is raw and honest, reflecting the intensity of the emotions being expressed. The use of first-person narrative creates a strong sense of immediacy and empathy.

The moral lesson of the poem is a testament to the power of hope and faith. Despite the darkness of his situation, the protagonist finds solace in his belief in a higher power. The poem serves as a reminder of the human capacity for endurance and the importance of perseverance in the face of adversity.

The Saints

And they call themselves saints!
Saints of Corinth or saints of Galatia?
Show me your master, and I'll mention your name.
Lucipher's disciples, saints of darkness!
Undercover soldiers, your origin hidden;
Bible in hand, hunting every nook
To find the lost lamb, the spiritual poor,
Into the house of the Lord, duty so obeyed.
Smiles, gifts and feigned goodness, your kindest gimmicks
To woo the spiritual poor
Into the house of the Lord, a house of den!
Church bell rings: ding-dong! Ding-dong!
Yelling to the saints to commune in the house;
Dressed in fine robes,
To meet the preacher in his finest robe.
With angelic and pleasant voices resonating through the house,
Hymns and choruses so wonderfully sang:
'Hallelujah! Hallelujah! Hallelujah! Glory be to God!'
Invitation to the divine spirit, miraculous works assured;
Like the Last Supper, savory meals abound
At every gathering, a joy to the spiritual poor;
Brother-in-Christ, Sister-in-Christ, divine titles of the saints.
Deception! Deception! Deception!
Deception to the spiritual poor,
Taint to the true saints,
Blasphemous to the Divine Spirit,
A mockery to the true LORD.

Corrupting the spiritual poor with your poison pill;
A pill of no return to the shepherd's fold.
Let's know your portion, and we'll thread with caution.
Like rockets, church towers rise so high in the skies;
Their polished skins, mirrors for the passers-by;
Inner kept kingly to keep the holy saints;
Shrines adored day and night;
Bullion and precious stone, their high prices.
The heart, God's only house, be kept like the towers,
Rejoicing Christ, at Heaven's High Table, will reward a prize.

Commentary:

The poem "The Saints" is a sarcastic critique of religious hypocrisy and the corruption of spiritual institutions. The central theme is the contrast between the outward appearance of piety and the inner reality of greed, deceit, and self-interest.

The poet employs vivid imagery and satirical language to expose the hypocrisy of the "saints." The diction is sharp and ironic, highlighting the discrepancy between the words and actions of the religious leaders. The use of biblical allusions, such as the reference to the Last Supper, adds depth and irony to the poem.

The moral lesson of the poem is a call for genuine spirituality and ethical behavior. The poet urges readers to question the motives of religious leaders and to seek true spiritual fulfillment through personal devotion and service to others. The poem serves as a reminder of the importance of discerning between true faith and false piety.

My Friends

My friends are my enemies,
And my enemies, my friends;
A fact none of us can overtly utter,
For we seem to be bound by an oath of secrecy
To protect our identities, the white and the red.
We see one another as enemies,
But we are still friends.

Like the tongue and the teeth in the same room,
We tread and walk together,
But far apart in hearts.
Perhaps, Heaven's design that we temporarily live together,
That we cannot escape from one another;
We play hide and seek in the same room,
But, awhile, meet to confront each other.

Friendship wrapped in enmity,
Or enmity shielded in friendship?
Pretence and false courtesies, features so common.
From the center, near and afar we'll have come together.
We sit together for knowledge with cheerful faces;
We dine and chat in seemingly good faith.
But fire is burning underneath.

Men and women, foot soldiers in pursuit.
In my presence, wearing masks of smiles, wickedness underneath;
Deadly traps set apart for their friendly foe!

Out of my fall comes their utmost joy,
With feigned consolation they reward me.
Duty so accomplished, a toast for the occasion.
But millions a time, victims of their own misdeeds.

They pretend to be my bosom friends,
But, indeed, they are heartless fiends.
They feign true friendship during the day,
But wage war in the night.
Oh, children of Jezebel! Children of darkness!
Failure were your traditional sex traps;
Narrow, but swift escapes so well-done!

What's my charge that I may plead?
Hatred without apparent cause or cure?
Invisible beings with venomous fangs, fireflies, bodies transfigured,
Eyes brighter than the sun, doing their master's will in darkness:
Disgrace, plunder and utter destruction.
They don't wink an eye a night,
Nor a respite a day.

Oh Saul, for how long can you pursue David, the anointed one?
Oh foes, when will you feel remorse and offer your olive branch?
When will you wear your sackcloth and ashes?
Wicked hearts know no repentance.
Your own bitter fruits will you eat.
But as my Creator lives maternal,
So shall I surely live eternal!

Commentary:

The poem "My Friends" delves into the complex and often paradoxical nature of human relationships, particularly those marked by both friendship and enmity. The central theme is the tension between appearance and reality, the mask of friendship concealing underlying hostility.

The poet uses direct description and a strong sense of irony to convey the message. The diction is both lyrical and biting, reflecting the emotional turmoil of the speaker. The use of biblical allusions, such as the reference to Saul and David, adds depth and historical resonance to the poem.

The moral lesson of the poem is a cautionary tale about the dangers of misplaced trust and the importance of discerning true intentions. The poet encourages readers to be vigilant and to guard against those who may harbor ill will. The poem also serves as a reminder of the enduring power of hope and faith, even in the face of adversity.

Lonely Man

I came to the world alone,
And so shall I leave this troubled earth alone!
In abundance of men do I walk alone;
From the very beginning does a man form it,
That he may alone earn his life.
Alone do I conceive my thoughts and form my judgments;
The maker of my world, the tailor of my destiny.
I sow and harvest my field alone;
Good yield, I grab with joy and grace;
Poor yield, I embrace with bitterness and disgrace.
A journey with unpredictable and unknown destination have I begun;
Rough, tortuous and winding, my cross behind me;
Full of darkness and without guide;
Mountains and slopes do I crawl and race;
Deviations and detours so common;
Enduring all the hardship and dangers awaiting a lonely traveler;
Like the chick, if a hunting hawk will whisk me away, I know not;
Whether my own faults will make me fall, I know not;
Whether a stray misfortune will hit me, I know not;
Fate holds the secret!
Alone do I endure whips of the sun and the rain;
A journey man seems to begin with life and hope,
But sometimes ends with sadness and despair.
But if Heaven pours on me grace and a shield,
Determination and perseverance will I wear on my neck,
That I'll win the lonely race.
No more pain and tears will I shed;

With greatest happiness will I receive the winner's prize,
And with joy, I'll wear my noble crown, endless.

Commentary:

The poem "Lonely Man" delves into the profound theme of human solitude and the individual journey through life. The central idea is that despite being surrounded by others, every individual ultimately faces their challenges and triumphs alone.

The poet employs a contemplative and introspective tone, using vivid imagery and powerful metaphors to convey the solitary nature of existence. The diction is both simple and evocative, striking a balance between accessibility and depth. The use of first-person narrative creates a strong sense of intimacy and personal reflection.

The moral lesson of the poem is a call for self-reliance and resilience. The poet encourages readers to embrace their individuality and to persevere in the face of adversity. The poem serves as a reminder that, while we may seek companionship and support, the ultimate responsibility for our lives lies with ourselves.

Grace, I'm Sorry!

"I don't know you!"

Vain, simplistic utterance my lips made.

Not hatred, not pride, not anger or discrimination,

But empty, unthinkable declaration, without a cause.

Sin, man's natural weakness, once committed, cannot be altered or justified;

Crime, once done, cannot be hidden forever.

To give it a sanctuary is a poison to the heart and the mind.

Thick clouds of self-reproach and heaviness control my thoughts;

Self-shame do I endure day and night.

The only compensation, and to set my mind free,

Equal measure of open confession do I make.

Please, no vengeance nor retribution!

For if there's any, I've already received it.

Urgent and genuine pardon do I humbly plead,

For I'm sincerely sorry!

Commentary:

The poem "Grace, I'm Sorry!" is a heartfelt expression of remorse and repentance. The central theme is the power of forgiveness and the importance of acknowledging one's mistakes.

The poet employs a sincere and contrite tone, using simple and direct language to convey his feelings. The diction is both humble and earnest, reflecting the speaker's genuine regret. The use of first-person narrative creates a strong sense of intimacy and vulnerability.

The moral lesson of the poem is the importance of owning up to one's mistakes and seeking forgiveness. The poet demonstrates the courage to admit wrongdoing and to ask for redemption. The poem serves as a reminder of the transformative power of forgiveness and the potential for personal growth and renewal.

Let My Enemies Speak!

Oh LORD, let my enemies speak out!
A true confession,
That I may be vindicated.
I've been silent, acquiesced,
That the truth may be hidden forever,
A cover-up for my enemies,
That I may be the victim of their secret plots.
My voice reaches no ear.
Branded a liar, a jester,
Who'll listen to me, a poor waif!
But you're my vindicator and redeemer,
The witness to my afflictions.
Let my enemies speak out,
And I'll have rest.

Commentary:

The poem "Let My Enemies Speak!" is a plea for justice and vindication. The central theme is the frustration and despair of a person who has been falsely accused and silenced.

The poet employs a somber and pleading tone, using simple and direct language to convey his distress. The diction is both powerful and vulnerable, reflecting the speaker's emotional turmoil. The use of first-person narrative creates a strong sense of intimacy and personal connection.

The moral lesson of the poem is a reminder of the importance of truth and justice. The poet expresses a deep longing for vindication and a desire to expose the falsehoods of his accusers. The poem serves as a cautionary tale about the dangers of unchecked power and the importance of speaking truth to power.

Goodbye, Utsunomiya!

A simple countryman
In search of knowledge,
Welcomed in this humble earth.
With your fresh and inviting autumnal breeze,
I trod on your bare chest to make myself good.
My temporary stay in this land,
Both Adam's Paradise and the Hades;
I won and lost!
But my gain, a profitable enterprise for my future's mission.
But *your* treatment, whether kind or cruel,
Not in my jurisdiction to pass judgment,
For no stranger's purview to score marks for his hostess's performance.
The people I left behind: some deserve honor, others deserve rebuke,
Or vengeance?
Genuine treatment, embraced and honored,
But treacherous benevolence,
A kiss to kill.
My departure, not out of outrage,
But a threshold of life in the offing;
To pursue the mission undone.
The recipient's noble appreciation,
Always a thank to his giver,
The veneration of the heart, mind and spirit.
If our relationship has come to an unplanned end
At *your* command,
Let me say, *adieu!* to you.

While I cross into Suzumenomiya and your glittering lights fade
　behind me,
In a calm, solemn emotion, my eyes benignly humbled before you,
I'll gently open my lips in a quiet ceremony,
Between a hostess and her guest,
And say, 'Goodbye!'

Commentary:

The poem "Goodbye, Utsunomiya!" is a reflective piece that explores themes of gratitude, disappointment, and the bittersweet nature of farewell. The central theme is the complex interplay between human connection and personal growth.

　The poet employs a contemplative and introspective tone, using vivid imagery and sensory details to evoke a sense of place. The diction is both simple and evocative, striking a balance between accessibility and depth. The use of first-person narrative creates a strong sense of personal connection and emotional resonance.

　The moral lesson of the poem is a reminder of the impermanence of human relationships and the importance of gratitude. The poet acknowledges both the positive and negative experiences encountered during his time in Utsunomiya, expressing gratitude for the opportunities and lessons learned. The poem serves as a reminder of the importance of cherishing the present moment and letting go of the past.

#202

Lured into *that number*, that dark cubicle,
The intended place of my rest
Became a place of my arrest,
A place of horror, mental torture and perversion;
From white to red, vain attempt to change the unchangeable;
Dictating deceit, insults and threat of death;
Locked and fettered in the dark cell,
That I would not see the light of the day.
Not a monk nor a hermit, but a prisoner of the devil.
Bread and wine, their unsuccessful weapon.
But who can limit the Omni-potent hands of my Creator?
For His immeasurable love, He caused my freedom;
The gate of Auschwitz Birkenau camp finally opened;
My enemies, once demons on rampage now on the run.
The invisible, not invincible after all!
They scattered and scampered.

My faithful Father, what shall I say unto you?
And what shall I do in return?
Who, *who* is like Thee?
Can I ever finish praising your Holy Name?
What you've decreed, no one can change;
Whom you've anointed, no one can touch;
Not only for Job and Daniel your grace was lent;
You waged the fight where I could not stand.
You comforted me and wiped out my tears;
You made my enemies bow their heads in perpetual shame and pain;

Your greater works transpire forever,
And your miracles, unending for your loved.
Your caring eyes and shelter, always upon your children;
Everlasting protection rests assured,
That your Holy Name be glorified.
My life, a living gift unto you forever!

Commentary:

The poem "#202" is a powerful and poignant reflection on the experience of imprisonment and the ultimate triumph of hope and faith. The central theme is the resilience of the human spirit in the face of adversity and the power of divine intervention.

The poet uses vivid imagery and emotive language to convey the horrors of captivity. The diction is both stark and hopeful, reflecting the depths of the speaker's suffering and the strength of his faith. The use of first-person narrative creates a strong sense of intimacy and personal connection.

The moral lesson of the poem is a testament to the enduring power of hope and the importance of faith in God. The poet expresses gratitude for his deliverance and acknowledges the divine hand in his liberation. The poem serves as a reminder of the human capacity for resilience and the transformative power of faith.

The Rising Sun

When I wake up in the morning,
And see your maiden light,
Like the lily by the river,
Like your blossom flower Oshimazakura in the Spring,
My centuries' old worries dissipate.
You're far from the world,
But from the East you illuminate the world.
Rich in both mind and countenance;
Gentle in manners, humble in conduct;
You don't burn, bark or scatter.
Home far from home, you keep warm and draw to yourself.
High above the world.
Who, who is like you?
Who created you?
Who molded you?
My palm in His palm
To show my appreciation for His aesthetic prowess.
Your tender touch, comfort to the poor;
Touch me, caress me;
Uh, what a sweet sensation every man'll gamble with his life!
Stay well, stay blessed
With love!

Commentary:

The poem "The Rising Sun" is a beautiful ode to Japan, celebrating its cultural heritage, natural beauty, and peaceful spirit. The central theme is admiration for the country's unique identity and its positive influence on the world.

The poet employs a strong description and sensory details to evoke a sense of awe and wonder. The diction is poetic and evocative, reflecting the speaker's deep appreciation for Japan's beauty and culture. The use of first-person narrative creates a strong sense of personal connection and emotional attachment.

The moral lesson of the poem is a celebration of cultural diversity and the beauty of different ways of life. The poet highlights the importance of appreciating and respecting other cultures, particularly those that offer unique perspectives and values. The poem serves as a reminder of the interconnectedness of humanity and the power of cross-cultural understanding.

Kings and Kinsmen

I could remember,
I could remember those dark days in the black soils.
I could remember the abominable and shameful acts of the stool
    and the skin;
The devil's stool and skin.
Like their lesser gods, their names too sacrilegious to mention;
Hands lifted up for a majestic walk,
Wrapped and clad themselves in brocades, praise and appellations
    undeserved.
Relying on dead and useless images for their counsel,
Thus, betraying their own wisdom and intelligence.
Oh kinsmen, the source and the beginning of your woes!

Owners and masters of the land, turning the palace into a house
    of horror;
Hands peeled to bones for their deadly dance, the source of
    their entertainment;
Executioners, shedding the blood of innocent victims—their own
    human kind,
In great fear and horror;
The unholy and abominable sacrifice to their dead and useless images;
Men castrated and turned into women: a crime against kinsmen and
    their Creator;
Using lies, fear of the unknown and intimidation to suppress their victims;
Leaders without insight; corrupt and wicked minds,
Where were your oaths you swore to your kinsmen?
What were their sins to deserve these untold treatments?

Bad shepherds, giving their flock to the greedy wolves for a tot of wine;
Without guns and spears, the greedy murderers, who could not discern right from wrong,
Caused atrocities against the innocent kinsmen;
Allowing the enemy to rape and murder the maidens in your own lands;
The murderers made them oversee their kinsmen leave the hinterland and shores without a squirm or reproach,
Into perpetual slavery, pain and death!
Marks in their skins, spit in their faces, culminating in their degeneration,
And their legacy: permanently changing their fate and destiny.
Greed and simplemindedness made them servants before aliens on their own lands;
It was moments of ugliness; simplemindedness and wickedness that stole the show!
The entrusted custodians, symbol of cultures and identities,
Now flirting and tainting their names and titles with names of alien cultures;
Crowns of shame!
And using the peoples' treasures for their own pleasures.
For their greed, the stool and the skin put on auction, heir-apparent denied.
In transition, a time to leave the scene is near.
Like the chuff, so shall their end come to pass,
For they've outlived their usefulness.
Let the times fade with them, the wind sweeping them afar,
That they rule no more!

Commentary:

The poem "Kings and Kinsmen" is a scathing critique of the corrupt and oppressive leadership of traditional African rulers. The central theme is the betrayal of trust, the abuse of power, and the devastating consequences of such actions.

The poet employs impactful descriptions and cutting language to convey the brutality and injustice of the rulers' actions. The diction is both lyrical and scathing, reflecting the speaker's deep anger and disappointment. The use of historical references and cultural symbolism adds depth and resonance to the poem.

The moral lesson of the poem is a call for accountability and justice. The poet urges the people to reject the corrupt leadership and to demand a more equitable and just society. The poem serves as a reminder of the importance of good governance and the dangers of abuse of power. It also highlights the enduring legacy of historical injustice and the need for reconciliation and healing.

Citizen

The tribe of the world,
I do not belong;
Heavenly citizenry do I hold.
A stranger, the tribe does not know me;
The tribe of Adam, the tribe of darkness,
Sin so sweetest on their tongues;
A detour from it is an abomination.
Their beauty is ugly and their wisdom, utter foolishness.
They champion vanity and rottenness and condemn virtue,
Wreaking their own existence with chaos and disorder.
Children of the law, the unbending stick;
Their statutes and judgments lead to dead end,
Leaving no one safe, both the maker and the subject.
Christ's ambassador, being treated like a convict,
Brotherhood of the grape,
Pursuing your little Joseph with all your heart and mind;
Blood murders blood with hate and arrogance.
My navel cut off from my roots,
And planted deep among children of the Rising Sun,
My temporary home,
To fulfill my Father's great mission.
Pains, shame and irritation have I endured;
Wickedness and despise have I suffered.
Yearning to leave for my Father's home, where I belong;
Yearning to be among the Holy Family, the saints and the holy angels,
Worshipping the great Throne with joy and in one accord;
My Father's glory, the source of light,

Pure gold shining all day, peace and happiness unlimited;
My Father's home, my natural home,
Will I rest and rejoice eternal.

Commentary:

The poem "Citizen" delves into the theme of spiritual alienation and the longing for divine connection. The central idea is the contrast between worldly existence and heavenly aspiration.

The poet employs a contemplative and introspective tone, using vivid imagery and powerful metaphors to convey his spiritual longing. The diction is both lyrical and evocative, reflecting the speaker's deep faith and longing for divine communion. The use of first-person narrative creates a strong sense of personal connection and emotional intensity.

The moral lesson of the poem is a call to seek a higher purpose and to strive for spiritual enlightenment. The speaker encourages readers to reject worldly distractions and to focus on their eternal destiny. The poem serves as a reminder of the importance of faith, hope, and the pursuit of divine grace.

In the Wilderness

The chronicles of my woes:
Things experienced and seen in the wilderness,
The wickedness of the devil and the filth of men intertwined.
Stripped naked, my captors drove me away in a cold wintry sleet
Into a quiet cell for a respite.
Homeless and by the street, my eyes pried into unknown faces for
 undeserved favor;
A priceless slave, I labored in vain at the devil's seat,
Where men'd turned into women and women into men—
Absurdity of life fully displayed.
Oblivious, they rendered their utmost secrecy into openness;
A warning to the living that nothing can be hidden forever under
 the Sun.
The 'Imperial' Cuss, surrounding himself with dead and
 useless images,
Forgetting his Creator and projecting himself into a god
To be worshipped and feared.
Oh man, remember you're mortal!
I fled with fear and hate.
A waif, I slept at a corner with the sky being my roof;
Begging fellow kinsmen for my daily bread,
Few accepting me with sympathy, many rejecting me with indignity;
It takes the mercy of God to receive undeserved favor from
 a fellow man,
For the prim and eccentric heart of man will never permit it!
I dogged my petty master, the cheat and vainly proud, just for a cent;
I slipped through the law of the land by hair's breath.

I've passed through wicked hands, hardship untold;
I've passed through dangerous paths for the sake of Christ.
But my woes, negligible of the earlier saints':
Painful deaths on the cross;
Brutal slayings by the devil;
Being buried alive.
Nothing can be compared unto these.
For the pains of the contemporary saints are blessings in disguise.
For the fourteen seasons' suffering,
Lessons taught, lessons learned,
Heralding the great mission in the offing,
That I may understand the world I live in,
That I become diligent in all things; not to be overtaken
    by circumstances.
For the successful completion of the course, victory is mine.
Unto my Father, my Enabler and Strengthener,
Whose handiworks are always perfect,
Be the glory forever more!

Commentary:

    The poem "In the Wilderness" is a poignant exploration of human suffering, resilience, and spiritual growth. The central theme is the transformative power of adversity and the ultimate triumph of faith.

    The poet utilizes strong illustrations and emotive language to convey the harsh realities of the speaker's experiences. The diction is both raw and poetic, reflecting the intensity of the emotions being expressed. The use of first-person narrative creates a strong sense of intimacy and personal connection.

    The moral lesson of the poem is a reminder of the importance of perseverance and faith in the face of adversity. The speaker's experiences have shaped his character and deepened his spiritual understanding. The poem serves as a testament to the human capacity for resilience and the power of divine grace.

The Fall of the Enemy

The enemy of old, my captor and tormentor;
The impersonator of Christ has fallen a great fall!
Your true identity hidden, spirit of the seas or space?
Without cause, you pursued me even in my cradle;
Without cause, you set deadly traps all around me;
You controlled my mind and thoughts in the world of darkness;
You made me suffer want and opprobrium before men;
Illness, threat of death and wretchedness became my lot;
Day and night, you and your league caused me harm.
But I've been delivered from you and underlings;
I've been set free from all things evil.
Enemy of old, you've fallen a great fall
To reveal the presence and rise of Christ in me,
And your evil works have been brought to an end,
And you'll be remembered no more!
Thanks be to Jesus Christ my Savior,
That I do not live my life for and by myself;
I live for Him Who created me, my LORD!
By this, He set me free from the devil and slavery;
My Advocate, He speaks and acts on my behalf;
His redemptive hands are always upon me,
And has delivered me from bondage and curses;
Christ, my Healer, has healed me from all diseases;
He guides me, the blind, to walk the earth and overcome
Its hurdles, dark corridors, ravines and tortuous winds;
He's restored me to my fortunes according to His will;
His anointing has clothed me like a garment,

Overflowing my body as I walk in His grace and glory;
He's brought me up in His wisdom and insights;
He's projected me high to manifest His glory;
He's provided me with great wealth and pleasure;
My comfort and happiness are without measure;
His grace and favor always upon me.
I'm a witness of Christ; have seen Him with my eyes,
And interacted with Him.
He's alive and active, working to save His saints;
My enemies are His enemies;
Woe unto those who want to cause me harm,
For he who touches me touches Him;
They can't escape the anger of Christ.
I'll sing praises to Him; He who made me;
I'll praise His Holy name as long as I live;
He who lives in Him lives forever!

I've shed the old self, now a new being!
For I've seen the Light in His purest form.
The greatest thing in a man's life is to win Christ.
For there is nothing more than this;
My physical life or death, in happiness or pain is secondary,
For Christ is enough for me.
Loving me more than I love myself,
He lives in me and I in Him,
That the unbreakable bond between us is justified.

Commentary:

The poem "The Fall of the Enemy" is a powerful celebration of spiritual victory and divine deliverance. The central theme is the triumph of good over evil and the transformative power of faith.

The poet uses striking imagery and touching language to convey the intensity of the spiritual battle. The diction is both lyrical and forceful, reflecting the speaker's deep faith and gratitude. The use of first-person narrative creates a strong sense of personal connection and emotional intensity.

The moral lesson of the poem is a reminder of the importance of faith and perseverance. The speaker's experience of suffering and oppression has deepened his spiritual understanding and strengthened his relationship with God. The poem serves as a testament to the power of divine grace and the ultimate victory of good over evil.

Ayumi

Woman is love!
A necessity for every living man.
Except the pious in divine holiness!
Adam did not know one,
And yet, he cried aloud for this noble gift,
That his life be complete and fulfilling.
For this, this centuries' old custom'll ever remain in a man's life.
In the deepest thought of the word,
The pair becomes deaf and insane,
For there is no wisdom in love.
There is no other world, except the couple's paradise,
Taking deadly oaths unimaginable,
Singing the love song in unison,
Sharing their thoughts and feelings,
And humbly surrendering the most secret of their flesh to each other,
For one owns the other.
The lovers' tiffs, the sweet pains,
And the tiny, piercing cry from a lovely little stranger,
The joy, the pride of the groom and his bride,
For woman is life!

Lonely, *wandering and wandering* in search of love,
Countless encounters in the woman-world,
The black and chocolate, symphony of rile and strife;
The brunette, parallel in thought and fashion;
The Caucasian, not in harmony!
Trying hard to find the nearest match,

But in my destitute, I found none.
Then entered the oriental orchard—the yellow and tan.
Oh, precious gift! With pleasure did I receive you, without toil.
Now you're mine, and me yours forever!

Spring life have we begun with its fresh, blossom greenery.
The beauty of Ichiyo, Oshimazakura and Kanzan!
Blessed Mary, let your lifestyle be sweet-scented,
Your progeny, a blessing unto the world;
In my distress, let your humor comfort me;
In contrast to Eve, draw me closer to my Creator,
That my crowns be magnified,
For woman is glory!
The Creator's gracious choice, a humble, perfect match,
Ayumi, you're blessed!

Commentary:

The poem "Ayumi" is a celebration of love, marriage, and the beauty of the feminine form. The central theme is the transformative power of love and the importance of finding a soulmate.

The poet uses rich descriptions and poignant language to convey the intensity of his feelings. The diction is both lyrical and passionate, reflecting the speaker's deep love and admiration for his partner. The use of first-person narrative creates a strong sense of intimacy and personal connection.

The moral lesson of the poem is a reminder of the importance of cherishing love and appreciating the beauty of human relationships. The poet emphasizes the significance of finding a partner who complements and uplifts one's life. The poem also celebrates the diversity of human beauty and the power of love to transcend cultural and societal boundaries.

The Great Escape: A Lament for Lost Worlds

The contents of creation are hidden from men,
Lest he claim ownership and become boastful.
Man's knowledge overflows its brims,
But infinitesimal of nature's whole.
People of Babylon, the stubborn generation, have come again!
Nimrods, building their tower far beyond the skies,
The speedy, flying craft and gadgets, the aerial monuments,
The foolishness of men once again displayed!
Stubborn hearts, treading and acquiring beyond your habitat is a trespass!
Woe unto the world and its inhabitants; he who pursues this unholy mission!
The great tower did not fall alone; the fragment of the tongue,
And their friction has not left the world safe.
But this, the simplest enduring result.
A shell, Satan has filled him for his purpose;
Their tools and knowledge, the devil's provisions;
The eye cannot see, the ear cannot hear, the heart cannot change,
Making them forget the existence and power of their Creator.
Custodians, their portion and stake in nature, self-destroyed,
Turning the earth into an irreplaceable dark hole,
Now in dire search of a heaven to live in.
Oh, who'll deliver this counsel unto men,
That their acts are foolish unto their Creator?
Who'll prompt man of his past, the rise and fall of the great tower?
And when will men learn wisdom?
Time spent, time wasted, tiresome and self-ridiculed,
For their works will come to nothing.

Commentary:

The poem centers around a critique of humanity's hubris and its destructive impact on the environment. It warns against the dangers of unchecked technological advancement and the exploitation of natural resources, emphasizing the need for humility and respect for the natural world. The title, "The Great Escape: A Lament for Lost Worlds," subtly suggests that humanity, in its pursuit of technological dominance, may ultimately be forced to become "planetary migrants" due to the environmental damage it inflicts upon Earth.

The poem employs a mix of elevated and colloquial language. Words like "Babylon," "Nimrod," "Custodians," and "irreplaceable" lend a sense of gravitas and historical resonance. However, phrases like "speedy, flying craft" and "the devil's provisions" maintain a contemporary edge, grounding the poem in present-day concerns.

The poem utilizes a prophetic and cautionary tone. It employs vivid imagery, such as the "tower far beyond the skies" and the "irreplaceable dark hole," to depict the potential consequences of humanity's unchecked ambition. The use of biblical allusions, like the reference to the Tower of Babel, adds a layer of historical and mythological significance.

The poem serves as a stark warning about the dangers of environmental destruction and the importance of ecological responsibility. It encourages readers to question the prevailing paradigm of technological progress and to consider the long-term consequences of our actions. The poem ultimately calls for a return to humility, a deeper understanding of our place in the natural world, and a commitment to living in harmony with the environment.

The poem resonates with contemporary concerns about climate change, environmental degradation, and the search for alternative habitats beyond Earth. It serves as a poignant reminder that while technological advancement can bring progress, it must be pursued with a deep respect for the planet and a long-term vision for sustainability. It also emphasizes the enduring power of faith and the need to connect with something greater than oneself.

Matchmaker

I knew you nowhere,
But you took me somewhere.
A medium, your duty timely accomplished.
A perfect match in its very best,
A turning point in my life.
Loving me, loving you: the core of friendship.
But our association kept in perpetual distance;
The world and its culture run parallel to our path;
Life and its demand, a fence to our meeting.
The East and the West, two conflicting worlds do we live in.
A brief embrace, torn apart for good, separation worth mourning!
But the sweet memories of our past still hold us together,
The living pillar of our union.
Our meeting forbidden,
But for your contribution to my life,
My acknowledgement always in my lips,
Singing it all day,
Well done, Yuji!

Commentary:

The poem "Matchmaker" explores the themes of love, loss, and the power of human connection. The central theme is the bittersweet nature of long-distance relationships and the enduring power of friendship.

The poet employs a reflective and wistful tone, using vivid imagery and sensory details to evoke a sense of longing and nostalgia. The diction is both lyrical and poignant, reflecting the speaker's deep emotions. The use of first-person narrative creates a strong sense of intimacy and personal connection.

The moral lesson of the poem is a celebration of the enduring power of human connection and the importance of cherishing relationships, even when distance separates people. The poem serves as a reminder of the importance of gratitude and appreciation for those who have positively impacted our lives.

My Reign

Crowns are worn by the destined,
But he who wears the crown carries the crowd.
For they're inseparable, the cause of glory and challenges.
Woe unto him, who is born great, for his burden is great!
For the impermanence of life, many a great man has come and gone;
For the weakness of the flesh, their lives mixed with glory, and even gory.
Their fall, once at the beginning, middle or end,
Most seeing their rise before their fall.
But I've witnessed my fall before my rise.
Thus, my beginning in contrast to my end.
A fresh start have I begun;
My burden far behind me, happiness and glory ahead.
While the future is revealed unto me, my very self, I know not,
For my identity hidden from me.
My life carefully crafted and kept in a Heaven's vault,
Being revealed unto me in trickles, bits by bits,
That, perhaps, I boast not;
That nothing tampers with the mission set before me.
Life thrives between the past and the future, the present is temporary.
Father, let my reign turn to be good,
And your glory spanning the rest of my days,
Glittering like the stars,
Until I am gone.

Commentary:

The poem "My Reign" delves into themes of destiny, humility, and divine purpose. The central theme is the transient nature of earthly power and the importance of spiritual fulfillment.

The poet employs a reflective and contemplative tone, using vivid imagery and powerful metaphors to convey his thoughts. The diction is both lyrical and philosophical, reflecting the speaker's deep contemplation of life's mysteries. The use of first-person narrative creates a strong sense of personal connection and emotional intensity.

The moral lesson of the poem is a reminder of the importance of humility and gratitude. The speaker acknowledges the limitations of human power and the ultimate authority of a higher power. The poem serves as a call to live a life of purpose and to seek spiritual fulfillment.

Takahara

In the narrow walls of Takahara,
There I climbed and discerned forth:
One, two, three; three, two, one.

My steps echoing through the passage,
A meaningful disturbance for my cause;
The war on life continued.

A shield, you secured me in your pouch to remain unseen;
Uncovered alien, you kept me comforted and bold;
    my soul rest assured;
The law and the manacle finely escaped!

A nest, you nursed and kept me in absolute, solemn peace.
From a tedious hustle and bustle of the day,
I sprawled in your chamber for my daily rest.

I knew my departure would make me an orphan.
But I couldn't live with you forever;
I'd be off against your will.

A host, your primary duty had to continue unbroken;
Your chamber abandoned to play its role,
That the seller and the buyers'd look to you for their daily deal.

My leave for another haven might send me afar,
Missing you for a time prolonged.
But awhile, I'd return to you for our happy embrace.

Commentary:

The poem "Takahara" revolves around the theme of finding refuge and experiencing temporary sanctuary. It explores the emotional connection between the speaker, an illegal migrant, and the place he found shelter in—the third floor of the Takahara building in Tokyo, Japan. This place, a small, hidden shop, provides a sense of security and respite from the dangers and hardships he faces.

The diction is simple yet evocative. Words like "narrow walls," "climbed and discerned," "echoing," "secured," "nest," and "hustle and bustle" create vivid imagery of the speaker's confined yet comfortable existence within Takahara building. Phrases like "war on life" and "uncovered alien" subtly hint at the speaker's precarious situation and the constant struggle for survival.

The poem employs a reflective and intimate tone. The first-person narrative allows readers to connect with the speaker's emotions and experiences. The use of short, concise sentences creates a sense of urgency and a focus on the essential elements of the speaker's experience. The poem's ending, with the image of a future return, leaves a sense of hope and longing, suggesting a deep emotional connection to the place.

The poem subtly touches upon the human need for refuge and the importance of finding safe havens in a world that can often be harsh and unforgiving. It highlights the resilience of the human spirit and the ability to find solace and strength in unexpected places. Additionally, the poem implicitly addresses the plight of migrants and the challenges they face in seeking a better life.

"Takahara" is a poignant and evocative poem that explores themes of refuge, resilience, and the human need for connection. Through simple yet powerful imagery and a reflective tone, the poem offers a glimpse into the experiences of those who are forced to live on the margins of society.

Mitsukari (Ayumi)

She found me leaning on a tree—alone,
In deep thought of centuries' separation.
In relief, she lifted her eyes at the budding Sun,
Her pains and worries in quick dissipation.
Like a wanderer, she'd tramped for years,
Searching every street and corner in pursuit of love renewal.
Pining all day in forlorn and grief,
Her slim body had grown slimmer;
Her white dress turned grimed and beige;
The sapphires and the pearls disappeared from her body;
Her hair drooped in shabby strands and wild.
A brief meeting of our eyes,
But awhile, she was in flight;
Her long hair sizzling behind her;
The burden of remorse grisly pursuing her saintly heart;
She couldn't brace herself for the long separation between us.
But had my divine calling done us apart,
That I could fulfill my noble duty solo.
The job well done!
I groped my eyes through the moving crowd,
But she was gone!
I waded my way through the multitude,
Body bumps, murmuring protests,
Plodding every trail without a clue,
My weary body about to reject the holy cause in despair.
By providence did I find her in a nook;
Her slender body folded to herself,

Ruddy eyes closed for a rest; tears left their designs on her cheeks;
My uneasy, stretching hand lifted her up;
Her eyes lowered down, the tired humbled body leaned on me,
Pleading mercy for a sin undone.
Silent! Hands knitted together,
We ambled along in the bright, growing Sun
Into our home, the world behind us.
A new life'd begun in the process of re-union,
Timeless!

Commentary:

The poem "Mitsukari (Ayumi)" is a poignant exploration of love, loss, and the redemptive power of reunion. The central theme is the enduring nature of love and the transformative power of human connection.

The poet uses powerful imagery and emotive language to convey the intensity of the characters' emotions. The diction is both lyrical and passionate, reflecting the depth of their feelings. The use of first-person narrative creates a strong sense of intimacy and personal connection.

The moral lesson of the poem is a reminder of the importance of perseverance and hope in the face of adversity. The characters' unwavering belief in their love allows them to overcome obstacles and reunite. The poem also highlights the transformative power of love and the ability to transcend challenges through human connection.

Human Harvest

Infantrymen:
Wearing insignia of civilization and enlightenment,
They thread and wage bold and fearless.
Proud countrymen hail them at parade:
"Patriots; valiant; heroes; invincible!"
They're bred and fed with infernal hate,
Against fellow men: to kill and be killed,
The essence of the primitiveness of man,
Until the gun, their fetish, leads them to the grave.
Do we've to mourn the death of a warrior-in-action?
But pity and sorrow they deserve.
Oh poor warrior, fellow man's altered your destiny
For his pride and glory
In the shield of nationhood and defense;
Those who can make peace without a shot
Make life to have no meaning for a warrior.
They swear an oath to protect fortresses,
But they don't promise to lose their lives in a trice.
But death, once camouflaged in life, will soon be laid bare.
When the sun disappears and darkness falls;
When you hear the boom of the guns,
Cacophonies on the fields of Ukraine,
Deadly clashes and bloodbath,
Remember the harvest time has come.
The luckiest come home half-human, living dead!
They're cut and gathered in heaps;
Caskets adorned in national colors;

Stately requiem organized for the departed soul;
Soldierly portrait of a man in absence, now on show.
At his visage, widow and orphans shed unfinished tears;
Amaranth in their minds, he never fades!
Worshipped daily in false shrines and sanctuaries,
Warrior, do you've to die to live invisible?
Avoid it if you can,
For on this earth, life's lived but once!
Oh poor warrior, if your days've ended at a short,
Cenotaph: 'KNOWN BUT TO GOD!'
May your troubled soul rest in peace!

Commentary:

The poem "Human Harvest" is an emotional reflection on the human cost of war. The central theme is the senselessness of violence and the tragedy of human loss.

The poet employs vivid imagery and emotive language to convey the horrors of war. The diction is both lyrical and stark, reflecting the contrast between the idealization of soldiers and the harsh realities of combat.

The moral lesson of the poem is a call for peace and understanding. The poet questions the glorification of war and the sacrifice of human life. The poem serves as a reminder of the importance of diplomacy and the pursuit of peaceful solutions to conflict.

Reflections

The vanity tour in search of passion has ended,
The time to reflect on the fruitlessness of the romantic journey:
The thrills, drifts and rifts; the appointments and disappointments
At the three main virtual stations.
No need did I have for this indulgence,
For a soldier on a mission knows no luxury.
For my marriage, His divine promise as solid as a rock.
But the prolonged loneliness, Abrahamic impatience, my bane!
Man oh man, since ancient times, your indiscretion
And unbridled appetite for a single rib bone of yours
Has always been your woe!
Samson's misjudgment, Delilah's effect, eventually cost his life;
David's unquenchable lust led him to murder an innocent life;
Solomon's carnal proclivity, the cause of a divided kingdom.
The contemporary man isn't immune either:
The Clintonian obsessive eroticism; Kahnian sensual impulses;
    Woodian venereal addiction have consumed many a man,
With consequences manifold.
But I've escaped these and their perils,
Because Somebody else lives my life for me;
His Sovereign and absolute protection do I receive,
Or my retribution might have been weightier, a mother lode,
Perpetual repercussion even unto the world.

Commentary:

The poem "Reflections" is a contemplative exploration of human desire, temptation, and the importance of spiritual discipline. The central theme is the dangers of unchecked desire and the need for self-control.

The poet employs a reflective and introspective tone, using vivid imagery and powerful metaphors to convey his thoughts. The diction is both lyrical and philosophical, reflecting the speaker's deep contemplation of human nature and spiritual matters. The use of biblical allusions, such as the references to Samson, David, and Solomon, adds depth and historical resonance to the poem.

The moral lesson of the poem is a call for self-discipline and spiritual growth. The speaker acknowledges the seductive power of desire and the importance of resisting temptation. The poem serves as a reminder of the need to prioritize spiritual values and to seek divine guidance.

Manzanar

Poor aliens, driven by misery and deprivation
To far distant land for survival.
Like the wind, a hungry man knows no frontiers;
He braves inconceivable dangers at his peril,
Until he reaches land of abundance and hope.
But with repulsion, the host denies them his tended home,
Summons his kins, and steals their attention;
Infectious admonition to steep deep into their minds begins,
Then transforms into a creed—
Creed handed down from kins' generation to another immemorial;
It's worn like a badge: kins' badge of honor;
Creed that reminds and shapes individual kins' consciousness
Of the existence of a proud unique, enlightened caste among men;
Creed that's reset kins' mental configuration into oneness,
Setting them apart from "lowly and unequal lots";
Creed that's transformed individual kins into vigilantes of a sort;
Creed fixed on their lips like a balm that commands recitation:
"Devils in our midst; devils breathe out evil and damnation;
They don't belong here; don't belong to our breed
Of high pedigree, a rare kind among the living.
Duty bound to preserve our social purity.
Pinion them and they'll be weak;
Incarcerate them, and they can harm no more!"
A bounty put on each devil's head;
A reward for a vigilante's noble service.
Thus, the purge has begun:
Outcasts, abandoned on a country field East afar;

Their wails and travails suppressed
By the man-made skies and walls surrounding them.
Kept in compartmentalized cages and pens,
They live on rationed time and space
As though, nature has forfeited them so.
Animal farm, the farmer contents himself how he feeds his stock,
Permits measured piteous freedom, his grace!
In captivity, they're confined for centuries long;
Victims, their names and identities defiled;
Their lives laid bare and empty;
Their visages marked with grim and pathetic selves,
In perpetual penal subjugation and spite.
Innocent mournful souls, tortured minds, deaths!
Oh man, to be poor is a curse!
A sorrowful veil debasing the worth of man;
A sour on human conscience demeaning his sense of being.
It subjects him to the cruelty of fellow man.
Such has been their fate in the hands of their captors.
But let moral law judge the captor's path;
The light for humanity to behold right from wrong.

Commentary:

The poem "Manzanar" takes its title from the Manzanar War Relocation Center, a site in California where Japanese Americans and people of Japanese descent were detained during World War II (1942-1945). The poet uses Manzanar to symbolize the entire wartime relocation project undertaken by the US government. The poem alludes to this historical incarceration, drawing a parallel with the detention of migrants in contemporary Japanese immigration facilities by the Japanese government. The poet suggests that the experiences of these migrants and those of the Japanese detainees during World War II share key similarities:

1. **Similar Migration Patterns:** Despite the different time periods, both groups' migration is driven by poverty. Between 1890 and 1924, economic difficulties were the primary driver for Japanese people emigrating to the United States, where many found employment building railroads, in logging industries, and on farms. Certain individuals also went through the process to become naturalized American citizens. Similarly, unskilled migrants today seek better lives in Japan.
2. **"Us vs. Them" Mentality:** Both groups experience unhealthy social classification and the creation of an "us" and "them" divide, similar to the Japanese concepts of *uchi no hito* (insiders) and *soto no hito* (outsiders).
3. **Consequences of Discrimination:** This leads to racial discrimination, ill-treatment, and abuse. It evokes feelings of innocence and victimization in the sufferers and guilt and culpability in the host society.

The central theme is the dehumanization and suffering experienced by innocent migrants due to prejudice and fear.

The poet employs vivid imagery and emotive language to convey the harsh realities of incarceration. The diction is both lyrical and accusatory, reflecting the speaker's anger and frustration. The use of historical references and specific details adds authenticity and depth to the poem.

The moral lesson of the poem is a call for empathy, justice, and social responsibility. The poet urges readers to learn from the mistakes of the past and to work towards a more just and equitable society. The poem serves as a reminder of the importance of human rights and the dangers of prejudice and discrimination.

Baby King

Royal heavenly birth so divine!
Read the scriptures so foretold!
The Magi once led the joyous bliss;
Ever since has become a yearly norm.
Reindeer-sledges dredge the fielded snow;
Illuminations in starry forms adorn the world;
The Earth convenes a hurry happy Mass;
Saints humbly bow in praise and adulation;
Angelic sweet choruses fill the eager ears;
Merry in Heaven's gift of a Baby King;
Songs of joy and eternal love unto all men.
For the Savior of the world, Prince of peace is born.

Commentary:

The poem "Baby King" celebrates the birth of Jesus Christ and the significance of Christmas.

The poem centers around the celebration of Christmas and the birth of Jesus Christ as the Savior of mankind. It emphasizes themes of joy, peace, and hope.

The poem employs religious imagery and vocabulary, such as "Magi," "Reindeer-sledges," "Saints," "Angelic choruses," and "Prince of peace." The diction is both lyrical and celebratory, reflecting the joyous nature of the occasion.

The poem has a simple and direct style, making it easily accessible to a wide audience. The use of vivid imagery and sensory details, such as "Illuminations in starry forms" and "Angelic sweet choruses," creates a sense of wonder and awe.

The poem conveys a message of hope, peace, and goodwill toward all mankind. It emphasizes the importance of celebrating the birth of Jesus Christ and the values of love, compassion, and forgiveness.

Overall, "Baby King" is a traditional Christmas poem that beautifully captures the spirit of the holiday season.

No More Evidence

No more evidence do I need
To prove the existence of my Creator,
Having grown from believing in Him
To knowing Him in my life.
I'm sane and conscious of His dealings with me,
That I may not be judged wrong in my witnesses,
For they are certainly true, real and beholding.

No more evidence!
Not in dreams, trance or invisible realms.
But as the apostles and ancient saints lived with Him,
So do I!
Many a time have I met His Angels; twice have I met Moses;
Even when I am mean to them, they create and direct my paths,
Lest, I deviate from my course.
I met Him;
The encounter with my LORD Jesus Christ at a convenience store.
There, He took poverty away from my life;
Now, I'm a blessed happy soul flourished in prosperity!

No more evidence!
He provides my needs before I ask for them;
He shields me like a newborn baby,
Lest, I hurt myself;
He keeps my enemies at bay,
Or causes me to flee from them;
Now in exile, living Far East in a foreign land;

He heals all my diseases; now I'm a living whole!
He's redeemed me from a world I do not belong;
This world of darkness, pain and death, into light,
The assurance of life after death in perfect peace.
Personal loving and faithful Father,
He exists and lives eternal,
And those who seek Him in Christ will surely find Him!

Commentary:

The poem "No More Evidence" is a powerful testament to the speaker's unwavering faith in God.

The central theme is the speaker's profound and personal experience of God's presence and guidance in his life. It emphasizes the importance of faith and personal experience in understanding and connecting with the divine.

The poem employs a combination of simple, direct language and more evocative, spiritual terms. Phrases like "knowing Him in my life," "met His Angels," and "encounter with my LORD Jesus Christ" convey a sense of intimacy and personal experience.

The poem has a conversational and intimate tone, as if the speaker is sharing a deeply personal and transformative experience. The use of first-person narrative creates a strong sense of immediacy and authenticity.

The poem underscores the importance of personal faith and the transformative power of a relationship with God. It encourages readers to seek their own personal experiences of the divine and to cultivate a deeper connection to their faith. The poem also emphasizes the importance of trusting in God's guidance and experiencing the peace and joy that come from a life lived in accordance with His will.

Re-Union

Children of the Rising Sun,
Islanders of the Far East,
My dear beloved hosts,
On my thoughts and conscience'd your wrongs heavily laden.
But when I couldn't bear them any longer,
For shame and anger'd worn on me like a weathered rock,
And deep dejection had become my lot,
My love for you waned; my affection diminished.
I turned my back on you for a supposed indefinite while.
But my sad departure couldn't be for a mile.
In a very solemn remembrance, that, I Christian,
Beneficiary of ever-loving kindness and overflowing grace,
From moments in the womb, my cot days, now and forever,
Has my heart and mind transformed towards you in a race.
For divine benevolence requires me, the recipient,
To always treat humanity generous same.
Like a bridegroom loves his bride evermore,
Longing for an unending happy embrace,
So have I returned to love you even more,
For the loved must love.

Commentary:

The poem "Re-union" explores themes of forgiveness, reconciliation, and the enduring power of love.

The poem centers around the speaker's journey of self-reflection and his eventual return to a loving relationship with Japan. It highlights the importance of forgiveness, overcoming past grievances, and cherishing human connection.

The poem employs a blend of formal and colloquial language, creating a sense of intimacy and sincerity. Words like "benevolence," "grace," and "kindness" convey the speaker's deep appreciation and reverence for his God.

The poem has a reflective and introspective tone, with a focus on internal emotional states. The use of imagery and metaphor, such as the "burden" of past grievances and the "race" towards reconciliation, adds depth and emotional resonance to the poem.

The poem emphasizes the importance of forgiveness, compassion, and the cultivation of loving relationships. It suggests that even in the face of past hurts and disappointments, true love can endure and ultimately triumph. The poem serves as a reminder of the importance of cherishing human connection and striving for understanding and reconciliation.

The Last Apostle

Christ's beloved son,
His very true identity,
And symbol of His love for mankind,
He's the last apostle among them to die.
He ever lived, and yet, he lives once again!
He lives and walks the earth alone;
God's grace and favor are abundantly upon him.
For His kindness, He revealed unto him who he really is,
And hidden it from men.
Though, he may be lavished with pleasures after his work,
He has not come to eat and drink.
Just as he's come to mark the end of an era,
So has he come to mark the beginning of another.
He's been made to live in submissiveness and humility unto men,
And he's suffered in the hands of men a great deal.
He's been denied all things earthly;
Temporarily made a curse unto himself,
As though he is nothing among men,
That the world may reap the full benefits of his mission,
All things being perfected in Christ Jesus, his Employer,
Who's assigned and committed him to good works;
His Model, who denied Himself all things earthly,
Including His very life for the salvation of all men.
In spite of His endless power and greatness,
In humility He's born;
In humility He's painfully crucified;
In humility and glory, He's raised!

In all things he'll give praise to Him!
Glory be to God the Father and His beloved Son,
Amen!

Commentary:

The poem "The Last Apostle" explores the theme of discipleship, sacrifice, and the enduring legacy of Christ.

The poem focuses on the unique role and experiences of the "last apostle," a figure who embodies the principles of humility, service, and selfless dedication to Christ's mission. It highlights the importance of following Christ's example of humility and sacrifice in one's own life.

The poem employs religious imagery and vocabulary, such as "Christ's beloved son," "apostle," "salvation," and "God's grace and favor." The diction is both reverent and profound, reflecting the speaker's deep faith and reverence for Christ.

The poem has a contemplative and introspective tone, with a focus on the inner life and spiritual journey of the "last apostle." The use of biblical allusions and theological concepts adds depth and richness to the poem.

The poem encourages readers to emulate the example of Christ and his followers by living lives of humility, service, and self-sacrifice. It emphasizes the importance of prioritizing spiritual values over worldly possessions and striving to live a life that reflects the teachings of Christ. The poem serves as a reminder of the enduring power of faith and the importance of living a life of purpose and meaning.

Disclaimer of a Witness

I was looking, looking and looking
Until there was nothing else to see.
It was Mr. Button Man standing under a tree,
With his right hand over his shoulder, as usual.
That hand held something which accidently
Revealed itself to be a long knife.
For those of us who are interested in Mr. Button Man,
And what he does for a living,
He stands unmatched among men of his caliber.
He always wears a hood over his long face,
And wears a red cloak whether summer or winter,
Rain or shine, day or night.
How many of such coats he has is a mystery!
A man without a friend: seldom does he talk or smile.
He pulled the long knife from his back,
And headed northward, going where?
In that dead of a night?
He approached the Northgate where the rich old Gianni once lived.
He forced and entered *that* house; the door closed behind him.
I heard what seemed like a slit;
A brief whimpering sound followed,
And there was silence!
Immediately, I shivered back home to sleep.
The following day, Inglett, the caretaker of that house, was reported killed.
But please, don't call upon me to account for anything,
For I know nothing about Mr. Button Man,
And what he did that fateful night!

Commentary:

The poem "Disclaimer of a Witness" is a chilling account of a potential murder witnessed by the speaker.

The poem explores themes of guilt, fear, and the moral dilemmas of being an unwilling witness to a crime. It delves into the psychological impact of witnessing violence and the complexities of human conscience.

The poem employs a stark and minimalist style, creating a sense of tension and suspense. The use of vivid imagery, such as "long knife," "hood over his long face," and "dead of a night," evokes a sense of fear and unease. The diction is precise and deliberate, emphasizing the speaker's detached and almost clinical observation of the events.

The poem has a narrative structure, unfolding the events of the night in a suspenseful and almost detached manner. The speaker's voice is both observant and hesitant, creating a sense of ambiguity and uncertainty.

The poem raises profound questions about the nature of guilt, responsibility, and the limits of human knowledge. It explores the ethical dilemmas faced by individuals who witness acts of violence and the psychological impact of such experiences. The poem serves as a reminder of the complexities of human nature and the importance of confronting the darkness within ourselves and the world around us.

I Am Blessed

I'm the symbol of Christ's love for the world;
He knitted me out of His pure and endless love,
His illumination to shine forth in the darkness,
That He may be known unto the world.
The Son of the faithful and true living God,
I owe it utmost duty to proclaim Him,
His exceeding greatness unto the world.
The King's beloved son, I'm His fragrance unto the world;
I'm His witness, have met Him, spoken with Him;
Clothed in His glory, and always in His presence.
My very being is Christ, the Son of the faithful and true living God!
For His sake, He made me holy and saintly,
That the world may know Him as I know Him.
He's the light of the world, the Savior of the lost and the afflicted.
He absolutely possesses and commands all things;
His presence and authority stretch beyond spheres;
Land, seas, space and places hidden from men.
He gives me every good thing freely and abundantly;
Day by day, my strength is renewed by His breath;
Everything I touch with my hands becomes a blessing.
He's made me safer than the world put together,
And for this I fear no evil.
My enemies retreat and gaze in utter awe and bewilderment;
My adversaries quake with fear and proclaim aloud:
"What a Mighty God you have!"
The world cannot judge me whatsoever,
For I've been made immune to its laws and judgement.

He forgives me my sins even before I commit them,
For I live in the fulness of His eternal grace and love.
My Enabler, I can accomplish all things through Him.
Let the world worship and adore Him,
The Son of the faithful and true living God,
May His holy name be praised and glorified forever!

The good Shepherd of my life is Christ,
The Son of the faithful and true living God!
He knew me before I was conceived;
He designed me for His good works;
He cared for me even when I didn't know Him;
He opened my eyes for me to know Him.
I can never count my blessings;
Where do I begin? And where do I end?
For they're like the sand or the stars in the skies.
The King and His beloved son are inseparable;
He's my residence in whom I live;
Together, we live and reign with wisdom forever!
He admits me into His confidence, and abides in me
Knowledge of His great works, the riches of His creation,
The hidden truth and things yet to come.
I'm intoxicated with His perfect peace;
Heavenly peace the world does not know,
That I'm unconscious of the darkness around me;
When the dark clouds descend, the thunder strikes,
I'm blind and deaf to the devil's wicked constructions,
For they mean nothing to my joy and happiness in Christ.
In my actions and thoughts do I sin,
A filthy man deserving rejection and abandonment.
Yet, He draws me closer to Himself with His love;
With His blood, He cleanses and presents me blameless;
As He's holy, so has He made me holy!
If there's anybody I can believe in, it's Christ;

If there's anybody I can depend on, it's Christ;
If there's anybody I can boast of, it's Christ;
None can be compared unto Him;
I've overcome the world through Him;
The Son of the faithful and true living God,
May His holy name be praised and glorified forever!

I'm blessed, the beloved son of Christ,
Closest to the Savior than anybody else;
He was and is my LORD.
The Lamb, who presented Himself for holy sacrifice,
You're the source of my strength and enlightenment;
He who suffered, died and resurrected for our sake,
I'm blessed to be called your servant;
He who ascended into Heaven in unmatched glory,
I'm most honored to be appointed for your great commission;
He who sits at the right-hand side of His Father on the Throne,
Your divine purpose for my life is fulfilled;
He who will come with great power and glory,
Having prepared the way for your coming;
He who will judge the world with justice,
You have crowned me with your glory;
He who will make all things new,
I surrender myself unto you;
And establish His kingdom forever,
I live my life unto your glory;
The King enthroned to rule all His creation,
Sovereign LORD, may you reign forever!
The King who will rule His people with righteousness,
Gracious LORD, may your saints and Angels worship you forever!
In a world whose magnificence and glory has no precedence,
Holy Majesty, may you be praised forever!
A new happy life has begun,
Divine Holiness, may your will be done on Earth!

Fulfilling generations of prophesies,
Holy LORD, you are the beginning and the end!
My LORD come, come, come in your glory!
The Son of the faithful and true living God,
May your holy name be praised and glorified forever,
Amen!

Commentary:

This poem, "I am Blessed," is a profound and moving expression of deep faith and spiritual devotion.

The central theme revolves around the speaker's profound and intimate relationship with God, emphasizing themes of divine grace, salvation, and the transformative power of faith. It celebrates the speaker's personal experience of God's love, guidance, and protection.

The poem employs rich theological language, drawing heavily from Christian scripture and tradition. Words like "Christ," "Savior," "living God," "love," "glory," "kingdom," and "holy name" are used frequently, reflecting the deeply spiritual nature of the speaker's experience.

The poem has a lyrical and poetic style, with a strong emphasis on rhythm and rhyme. The use of repetition, such as "blessed" and "forever," reinforces the speaker's unwavering faith and profound gratitude. The structure of the poem moves from personal testimonies of God's grace to grand pronouncements of praise and worship, culminating in a powerful affirmation of Christ's sovereignty.

This poem serves as a powerful testament to the transformative power of faith. It encourages readers to seek a deeper relationship with God and to experience the joy and peace that comes from living a life dedicated to His service. The poem also highlights the importance of humility, gratitude, and unwavering trust in God's love and guidance.

This poem is a moving expression of deep spiritual conviction and a powerful reminder of the enduring power of faith.

www.ingramcontent.com/pod-product-compliance
Lightning Source LLC
Chambersburg PA
CBHW061501040426
42450CB00008B/1450